Berlin- matter of memory

Berlin- matter of memory
by Fredrik Torisson

First published in 2010 by

Ratatosk Publishing Ltd
66 Peabody Cottages
Rosendale Road
London SE24 9DP
United Kingdom

www.rttsk.com

Editor: Justina Bartoli

ISBN 10   0-9554632-1-1

ISBN 13   978-0-9554632-1-1

Printed in Germany

© 2010 Ratatosk Publishing Ltd
All rights reserved.

All illustrations (except p 120) copyright Ratatosk Publishing Ltd 2010

Berlin- matter of memory

Fredrik Torisson

Table of Contents

Introduction   page 9
    Monuments and relics   13

Part I- Monuments shaping Berlin's history   23
    A theory of ruin value   27
    The Berliner Stadtschloss   31
    Instant ruins at Tempelhof   43
    Berlin's bunkers   49
    The Topography of Terror   59
    The Holocaust Memorial   65
    Endnotes   77

Part II- The informal relics of Berlin   81
    The voids of the Berlin Wall   85
    A tale between two cities   97
    The Olympic Village of 1936   103
    Spreepark   113
    The Berg of Tempelhof   119
    Teufelsberg   123
    Endnotes   131

Introduction

There are many ways of getting to know a city. This book puts the spotlight on Berlin's relics and monuments and their role in a contemporary context. Relics are physical remains of the past, and monuments are physical embodiments of subjective historical interpretations. A fundamental distinction between relic and monument is intention. While the remains of a construction can generally be considered uninterpreted or unwritten, a monument is created and constructed as an interpretation of an event or an era.

In the context of this book, the term 'relic' refers to architectural relics: buildings, structures and their remains and ruins. The term is furthermore used as a juxtaposition to 'monument', which implies an explicit interpretation, a manufactured symbolism or significance. A monument is a "written" interpretation of history while a relic can be "read" and understood differently by different people.

It has often been said that monuments are manifestations of the current order of society. They may reveal the subconscious paths a society is taking, the unspoken and undeclared. This is particularly true in the case of Berlin. Berlin has been shaped by the 20th century to a greater extent than most contemporary European cities. An epicentre of world history from the early 1900s, Berlin was the stage for many of the conflicts and horrors that plagued the century. The city is filled with architectural relics from the Kaiser's reign, the Weimar Republic, the First World War, the Nazis, the Second World War, the Cold War, and finally, the reunification of East and West Germany.

Berlin's relationship to its own past is decidedly complex; there is a radical disparity in different groups' interpretation of Berlin's history, making each monument a statement, a compromise or a necessity.

Relics are different. Most of the relics described in this book are already half-forgotten. They are constructions that have not (yet) become monuments; some will one day undergo this metamorphosis and others will disappear. Berlin's relationship to its relics is no less complicated than the city's relationship to its past – defining what is worth preserving is a constant source of heated debate. Some periods are more or less consciously erased from the urban landscape, while others are considered more desirable and are emphasised to the extent that replicas of former buildings are constructed.

This book is both a discussion and an analysis of the fundamental difference between relics and monuments as well as the practice of turning relics into monuments in a wider historical context, not least with regard to authenticity.
It is also intended to call into question the development whereby some 20th century relics are meticulously erased while others become symbols and esteemed monuments.

The selection of relics and monuments portrayed in this book is, in a sense, arbitrary. Discovering and investigating them has been part of my getting to know the city of Berlin. However subjective the analyses, however without objective pretences, the fortunes and misfortunes of the relics and monuments depicted here will provide the reader with an intimate image of Berlin.

The relics in this book range from the overgrown or even dematerialised to the most obvious of remains. The monuments are chosen based on contemporary relevance; often they are debated and contested monuments that reveal something about this city. The selection of portraits here was made in part with a focus on narrative, specifically on objects that present us with a story, and in part on objects that disclose something about Berlin. The selection is also made to complement and to a certain extent overlap history books and architecture-historical guidebooks to the city.

The combined image will provide the reader with a different perspective of the city, offering an in-depth exploration of Berlin's evolution, destruction, division, reunification and what that means today.

Images
p. 6: Teufelsberg's abandoned US Army base
p. 8: Nature reclaiming the asphalt of Tempelhof Airport

Monuments and relics

A city remembers its past in different ways, including recorded history and the memories of its inhabitants. The urban fabric, a city's houses and buildings, also remember the past in their own way, shaping the collective recollection of the past. Through its relics and monuments, the city records and recalls the decisive points of its history, in turn forming part of the city's collective identity.

The relic
Relics are typically objects or constructions of cultural or historical interest. In the case of architectural relics, they are generally made by humans. They are genuine physical connections between the past and the present which leave interpretations open to us.

Berlin played a central role throughout the 20th century. It was the backdrop for some of the most wildly megalomaniacal urban ideas and experiments, as well as some of the darkest events in human history. It was destroyed, rebuilt, divided and finally united again. Berlin is a city that has always been wary of the relic, well aware of its ambivalence and its power as a symbol. For instance, after Hitler's suicide at the end of the Second World War, his last loyal followers burnt his body to ensure that it would not be paraded around by the Allied Troops as a trophy. In turn, the Allied Troops excised Hitler's bunker, burying it and removing it from the records to avoid inadvertently creating a relic that could potentially be utilised as a symbol should the Nazi movement

ever be resurrected. Ironically, the motivation for both sides at this particular junction in history was essentially the same: both sides tried to erase the remains of the National Socialists to avoid leaving potentially powerful and therefore inconvenient relics.

As opposed to the monument, the relic is no obedient servant. The relic is a turncoat, representing different things to different people – it often can symbolise the exact opposite for two separate individuals. The relic is unpredictable. It possesses the power to integrate the past into the present, and the relic is therefore dangerous.

Relics make up a great part of the collective memory of a city. They are what reminds us of what happened – as opposed to monuments, which remind us what other people want to tell us happened. Relics are the physical remains of history – in a certain sense, they are history.

Relics also comprise a great part of a city's identity. They are the connection back in time to what defines who we are as a society today, which gives us insight into the public resistance to change in the built fabric often encountered if it involves tearing down relics. Our relationship with the city includes thousands of relics connected to memories in our minds, most of which are primarily meaningful on a personal level. But historic relics are significant for many, sometimes even all of us, thereby making up not only a vital part of our collective memory, but of our relationship with the city and its identity.

The monument

A monument is a space or an object created to tell us about history, as interpreted by the designer. In a sense, it is a time machine intended to remind us of a historical event or person as perceived by the monument's creator. Monuments tell us about history, relics are pieces of history.

It is essential to emphasise the artificial nature of the monument. A monument is created in retrospect; it is not only a way to commemorate, but also a tool used to write history, or at least to focus history in a particular direction.

Because of its particular history, many of the monuments erected in modern Germany are so-called *"Mahnmale"* – warning monuments – that serve to remind future generations of past atrocities. Warning monuments do exist in other countries as well, for example to serve as national apologies, such as the *Captured Africans Memorial* in Lancaster, but they are particularly abundant in Berlin.

Another function of the monument is to historicise the recent past. Throughout history, it has been quite common that the first thing a victorious army builds in a conquered city is a monument to its own victory. By constructing monuments, the recent past is made into history, recorded with the emphasis that the recorded event is no temporary setback but a fait accompli. Among the first things the Soviets built in Berlin after the end of World War II were two monuments celebrating the Soviet triumph over the National Socialists. The gargantuan *Sowjetisches Ehrenmal* (*Soviet War Memorial*) in Treptower Park is literally an enormous concretisation of the Soviet presence in Berlin.

Monuments can be used to remember events, but also to forget. Although seemingly built to remember a person or event, a monument can be used to transfer anxiety and guilt into stone rather than allow it to weigh down the hearts and minds of people. The creation of a monument can be used to allow people to forget and move on – the stones will remember so that people will not have to any more. Or more cynically: building a monument is often akin to jotting down a note in the collective notebook – look, we even wrote it down so we would not forget it.

In short, monuments are ambiguous structures. The purpose of the monument is not always clear, but monuments are never constructed without an objective.

Relics monumentalized
Currently, Berlin is going through a process whereby monuments replace relics, particularly those related to the Cold War. Berlin is keenly sensitive to the power and ambiguous nature of the relic, and it is perhaps only natural that recent relics are replaced with monuments in order to avoid an unfavourable interpretation of recent history.

The relics of the Cold War are little by little either being erased or monumentalised. One example of this is the fate of the Berlin Wall. Most of the wall was torn down in the turbulence of 1989, but some sections remained and became relics of the past.

Other relics have met a similar fate. The *Palast der Republik* (*Palace of the Republic*), constructed by the German Democratic Republic (GDR), for example, was torn down a few years ago to make space for a resurrected Prussian castle that had occupied the location prior to the war. On one hand, Berlin views the relics as wounds rather than remains and instinctively wants to heal the scars of the division. On the other hand, what West and East Berliners regard as scars or relics differ substantially, and the conversion of relics into monuments can not be explained entirely by a desire to heal the city. Monuments and relics serve very different purposes in the memory and as a consequence, the history, of a city.

The disparity between relics and monuments
Two distinct differences between relics and monuments can be observed. The first characteristic that distinguishes relics from monuments is that relics are remains, concrete objects that are open to the observer's interpretation, while monuments always are directed, much like films are directed. The builder's interpretation of the event being commemorated is communicated through the monument. In that sense, a relic is objective, i.e. open to interpretation, while a monument is a subjective interpretation.

The second basic difference between architectural relics and monuments is that relics keep the era or event they have come to symbolize current, anchoring it in the contemporary world and inviting the observer to view it as a part of the present rather than the past. A monument on the other hand severs that tie, pushing the commemorated event or person decisively into the past, anchoring it in history regardless of how current it may be. This is why we feel there is something 'off' when monuments are built to honour living persons; a duality arises and that person suddenly exists in history as well as in the present.

Replacing relics with monuments is a way of rewriting the past, of writing history in a way that suits the current order. A George Orwell quote from 1984 comes to mind:

"He who controls the past controls the future. He who controls the present controls the past."

A city of monuments is a city of abstracted interpretations of memories, while relics are concrete objects of history that are open to interpretation by us and by future generations. When Berlin replaces relics with monuments, it is attempting to rewrite its history in a way that is more agreeable and less open to interpretation. The Cold War years are currently getting the same treatment as the National Socialist years, but the question is whether one rewriting is as legitimate as the other. Erasing the monuments of the losing side in a war has been a common practice throughout history. However, in the case of the Cold War, the emphasis is on reunification, not conquest or triumph – making the replacement of relics with monuments a rather dubious undertaking. In a sense, Berlin is still suffering from a 20th century hangover, and relics keep the city from moving on. Replacing the city's relics with monuments may allow Berlin to go forward, to forget, and to leave the 20th century and face the 21st. Only time will tell.

Images
p. 12: Abandoned *Plattenbau* in the Olympic Village
p. 14-15: Void after the fall of the Berlin Wall, Pankow
p. 18-19: The Holocaust Memorial

Part I

Monuments shaping Berlin's history

Berlin is a disjointed, juxtaposed and above all heterogeneous city. Since its foundation, it has tried to forge an identity for itself. During some periods, Paris has been the role model, in others it has been London or Rome. The art- and architecture critic Karl Scheffler put it well in 1910: Berlin is a city condemned "forever to become and never to be". Berlin is truly a city of process; a city that is always going somewhere but never arriving and standing on its own in its own right.

The city has gone from being the seat of regional Prussian monarchs to the seat of the Kaiser of all of Germany. Later, during the National Socialist years, it became the projected world-capital Germania. After the war, which destroyed a large portion of Berlin, the city became the most prominent location for the two competing systems of communism and capitalism. Both attempted to weave their superiority into the urban fabric in different ways. The two regimes' visions for the city varied wildly over the decades. The GDR went from the rampant delusions of grandeur of Stalinallee to the denunciation of history in Marzahn and then back to historicism with the 1980's redevelopment of Unter den Linden. At the same time, West Berlin went from the futuristic optimism of the *Haus der Kulturen der Welt* and the Hansa district to the post-modern critical reconstruction of the city in the *International Building Exhibition*, the IBA, trying to heal the many gaping holes remaining from 1945.

All in all, in Berlin Utopian ideas have been heaped on top of each other, and their remains are often vis-à-vis across the street. Architecturally, Berlin is quite possibly one of the least coherent cities in existence, and forty years of being divided by a wall was no help. Instead of historical continuity, Berlin bears witness to a constant battle between different systems and different ideologies expressed in architecture.

After the Wall came down, a new development was initiated. Historic continuity was on top of the agenda and the city was to become a unified whole – the 20th century was virtually a bad dream to be forgotten. Prussian architecture was held up as the role model for the reunited city. Building regulations stipulated that windows should be oriented upright rather than horizontally and that the façades of new buildings should preferably be built in natural stone and in keeping with the style of the old Prussian architecture of the 18th and 19th centuries.

One central figure in this development was Hans Stimmann, who was appointed Building Director of Berlin in 1991. His credo can be summed up in the following quote: "Berlin's key concern is sustained historical development, which relates history and future to one another." In other words, in the spirit of 19th century art historian John Ruskin: development that connects past and future, conveniently skipping over the 20th century.

This fictional historical continuity is still a guiding principle in the planning of the city. It is the driving force behind the "reconstruction" of the *Berliner Stadtschloss* and it can be seen in countless façades across the city. It is an attempt to write a history for a city with a fragmented past; to erect a monument to a past that never was, a monument to a mythical former grandeur, reflected in contemporary architecture. It does not make sense – and yet it does not have to, since it embodies what many would like to believe.

Images
p. 24: A censored tombstone in St Nicolai cemtary

A theory of ruin value

Monuments are often regarded as articulations of the current social order, the naked expressions that those in charge wish to convey. This was certainly the case with the National Socialist Party and Hitler, who at one point described architecture as "the word in stone": his message transmitted through the monuments and buildings created. Architecture was a physical manifestation of his political philosophy. This built propaganda was primarily intended to manifest the power of the National Socialists (NS). It was meant to impress the power of the party and of Hitler onto visiting foreigners, but, more interestingly, on future generations.

Inspired by the ruins of Greece and Rome, Hitler and his chief architect Albert Speer created a "theory of ruins" that involved constructing buildings which would not only be impressive today, but would also form impressive ruins in a thousand years. Even if Hitler's plans should fail, he would still awe future generations with the controlled decay of his constructions. Architecture was to be constructed with a double purpose, for now and for in a thousand years, and in both instances, they should convey the message of Hitler and impose the greatness of his era onto the observer. The ideas may have been inspired by John Ruskin, who encouraged architects to consider their constructions not only in their contemporary context, but also as decaying ruins in the future, to consciously create an architectural legacy. As a result, durable stone was the material of choice for the architecture of the

NS regime. Thick stone walls remain from the antique cultures, but steel would rust, producing rather unimpressive ruins. Unlike the motivation for cultures of antiquity, the main objective was not durability and conservation, but romantic decay.

According to Speer, Hitler wanted to create a "bridge of tradition" to establish a historical bond with future generations. Seeing the remains of the NS years in this light explains the removal of the relics by a culture desperate to dissociate themselves from the NS years. From the demolishing of buildings to the censoring of tombstones, NS constructions and traces have been systematically erased since the end of the war. Ironically however, they are often too solidly constructed to remove, since they were intended to last a thousand years, and their ruin value is conveyed to present-day Germans in a different way than intended, whether they like it or not. Various approaches have been taken. Some monuments, like the SS-barracks under Teufelsberg, have been buried; others, such as the airport Tempelhof, have remained, but their symbolism has undergone a metamorphosis over the years and the buildings have taken on a different value for the general public. Still others have simply been converted to fill other functions. The *Hochbunker* in Reinhardtstrasse, for instance, is home to a private art collection.

Images
p. 28-29: The Olympic Stadium by Werner March, 1936

The Berliner Stadtschloss

Berlin's turbulent history culminated in the 20th century, virtually tearing the city apart several times. *The Berliner Stadtschloss*, or *Berlin City Palace*, has played a central role. The Stadtschloss is long gone, but efforts are underway to "reconstruct" it, or at least its surface, in order to create a continuous history for the fragmented Berlin, or perhaps to rewrite the history of the city with less focus on the 20th century.

Background- a tragedy in three acts

The *Berliner Stadtschloss* dates back to the origins of the city of Berlin. Its history can be divided into three separate acts which have shaped its fate up till now.

Act I

The *Berliner Stadtschloss* was constructed in the 16th century, when an earlier medieval castle was demolished to make space for the it. Some of the best preserved documentation of the *Stadtschloss* before the 18th century is by Nicodemus Tessin, the architect who would later design Stockholm's *Royal Palace*.

The *Stadtschloss* took on its final form during the 18th century, when Prussia was the rising star of the German Empire, and the first King of Prussia, Frederick I, sought to create a worthy capital for the new kingdom. The renowned architect and builder Andreas Schlüter was appointed to renovate the *Schloss* in Protestant-Baroque fashion, creating the famous courtyard.

The *Berliner Stadtschloss* continued to play a role in the Prussian and later German capital up until the Second World War. The building was heavily damaged by Allied bombings and burned quite badly. Neither the Soviets nor the GDR had any interest in resurrecting a symbol of the Prussian monarchy, and thus in 1950, the remains were demolished.

Nowadays, there is some controversy as to whether the palace was demolished on rational or political grounds. Advocates of the *Stadtschloss'* reconstruction claim that the structure was sound and had been demolished for political reasons, while others maintain that the demolition was an act of necessity.

Act II

The second act opens with the construction the *Palast der Republik* (PdR), the *Palace of the Republic*, in the middle of the 1970's. This building was to become the hub of East Berlin. The PdR housed an impressive range of functions, from the *Volkskammer* (the GDR parliament) to bowling alleys. The concept of its design was partly based on the then-new *Kulturhuset*, or *House of Culture*, in Stockholm.

The building itself was a giant box, its façades covered with bronze-coloured glass windows. It was designed by a team of architects led by Heinz Graffunder and Karl-Ernst Swora. The PdR was both loved and loathed in a typical Berlin fashion; it acquired the nickname *Erich (Honecker)'s Lamp Shop*, a reference to its imposing chandeliers. The building remained the hub of East Berlin until the fall of the Wall in 1989. It was in this building that the GDR parliament ratified the reunification.

However, in connection with the reunification, the West German authorities decided to purge the building of socialism as well as the asbestos, and by 1998 little more than the structure of the building remained. Advocates of the reconstruction of the *Stadtschloss* claim this was a rational decision, that the asbestos could not be removed without gutting the building. Their opponents, however, claim that this was a politically motivated action after the collapse of the GDR.

Act III

The curtain went up again in the beginning of 1993, when a lobby group advocating the reconstruction of the original *Stadtschloss* pulled off a terrific stunt – they built a Potemkin village of the *Stadtschloss'* façades on a scaffolding. Approximately half of the façades were actually built, and the reflection of the other half in the bronze mirrors of the PdR's windows completed the illusion. This triggered a lively debate on the future of the site. In the meantime, the asbestos removal was completed, leaving only the PdR's skeleton.

During the debate, the shell of the PdR became a cultural hub in Berlin yet again. For a number of years, temporary uses of the space included concerts, nightclubs and exhibitions. However, demolition began in 2006, and the Parliament decided – with the support of a great majority – to rebuild the old *Stadtschloss*.
Subsequently, the PdR was dismantled. Parts of the steel-structure were resurrected as part of the *Burj Khalifa* in Dubai, currently the tallest building in the world.

At present, the site of the future *Stadtschloss* is a well-kempt lawn in the absolute centre of Berlin. Flanking the lawn are two rectangular construction boxes: one is the info-box for the

reconstruction that advertises the future *Stadtschloss*, which is to be called the *Humboldt-Forum*.

The other box is the *Temporäre Kunsthalle*, a temporary art gallery space which will be removed once the reconstruction begins. The *Temporäre Kunsthalle* is an inside-out gallery – artwork is displayed on the façade as well as inside the construction. Artists are invited to use the building's façade as a canvas.

Recently, the debate was rekindled when the exhibiting artist at the *Temporäre Kunsthalle*, Bettina Pousttchi, opted to adorn the gallery's façade with the façades of the *Palast der Republik*. Thus, the third act ends in a stand-off between the two opposing boxes on their lawn. Meanwhile, most Berliners seem quite content with the lawn itself.

The *Stadtschloss*, what is reconstructed?

The first, and perhaps most important question is: can one reconstruct the *Stadstschloss*? The short answer is no.

Reconstruction of destroyed buildings is common across Europe. There are plenty of examples, including most of the old city in Dresden. The fundamental problem in this case is the lack of adequate documentation of the building to reconstruct it.

There are sufficient photographs documenting the building's façades, but the documentation of the interior is inadequate for a reconstruction in technical terms. In other words, the result will be a reconstructed set of façades rather than a building.

As a peculiar olive branch to those who advocated that a modern building should be built on the site, an architectural competition was held for one of the façades. This façade is to be built in "modern" style, while the rest of the façades will be reconstructed according to the 18th century Protestant-Baroque model.

The winner of the farcical competition was the Italian architect Francesco Stella. Having never heard of Stella, some of the larger architecture firms that had competed immediately discredited his competence, claiming that they should rightly have won the competition. The debate then developed into a lengthy court process.

Behind the façades, the interior of the *Humboldt-Forum* will be modern; the building is to be constructed with modern floor-plates and a modern interior. Some of the more prominent staircases and reception rooms will be reconstructed in a style resembling a simplified version of the original décor.

The structure's projected function appears to be of less importance than the building's façades. Among the suggestions have been a congress centre, several non-European museums and commercial venues to finance upkeep and construction costs, which are currently estimated at € 670 000 000. Even with the level of Private-Public investment imagined by the advocators, it is difficult to see how the project will be financed.

Taking the city of Berlin's economic situation into consideration, and in light of how recent developments in Berlin have turned out (*Hauptbahnhof*, the *Central Railway Station*, resembles a shopping mall more than a train station), it is not unlikely that the result will ultimately be more commercial than cultural. A shopping mall in the garb of the *Stadtschloss*, some fear.

Creating a past for the future

One of the most intriguing questions is *Why?* Why rebuild the façades of a lost palace at an enormous expense, why tear down one of the city's undeniably more historical buildings to make room for it?

Like any good drama, the answer is a complex mixture of nostalgia, vengeance and the dream of living happily ever after. The nicest way of looking at the motivations behind the reconstruction is to see it as a simple case of nostalgia. The *Stadtschloss* is thus a win-win project for the city and its inhabitants. The city will become somewhat more coherent, at least superficially; the *Schloss* will draw more tourists to Berlin and generate much-needed jobs, at the same time making money for its owners and operators. This is the vision presented by the advocates of the reconstruction.

A more sinister way of looking at the reconstruction is to regard it as another turn in the turbulent history of the site and the city. Pride demands vengeance for the demolition of the *Stadtschloss* and order restored. This is essentially the view of those who wanted to retain the PdR and are still mourning its destruction.

Yet another answer to the question presents itself if one looks at Berlin and the city's identity in a historical context. Berlin is full of attempted Utopian projects that were intended to forge an identity for the city. The Kings of Prussia, the National Socialists and the Socialists, among others all attempted to shape the city in their form. Each tried to create a stable, lasting order of society. Most efforts failed within fifty years, but the structures remain as elements of a city which is to a great degree comprised of failed Utopias piled on top of each other.

Technically, the reconstruction of the Stadtschloss could perhaps be regarded as another Utopian project, but one attempting to create a past rather than a future; a Utopia that creates a continuity of history that never really existed, a reworked history that everybody can be comfortable with, in that it omits the horrors of the 20th century. The reconstruction could be perceived as a return to an earlier idea of Germany, a Germany of which to be proud of rather than ashamed. Some have referred to it as a whitewash of history.

It is the dream of a past that never existed, where forms and symbols have been altered to suit contemporary ideas of society. The idea would aid the production of identity and unity based on an imagined past rather than an imagined future. Or rather, it would aid the production of a future identity based on the creation of a historical identity, in a very Orwellian fashion.

However, for most people today, this heap of failed Utopias *is* the identity of Berlin: a comprehensive, unified identity is not what Berlin is about; heterogeneity is what sets the city apart from other European capitals; the celebration of differences is the essential, inalienable freedom of this city. The attempt to create just another Utopia on top of the existing city only follows in this tradition, as will its failure, and its eventual absorption into the heterogeneous urban fabric.

Images
p. 34-35: The dismantling of the *Palast der Republik*, 2007
p. 38-39: *Temporäre Kunsthalle* with the façade of the *PdR*

Instant ruins at Tempelhof

Tempelhof has a short but dynamic history. The airport has symbolized several distinctly different things to Berlin, changing radically every twenty years or so. It was constructed in the 1930's as one of the world's first commercial airports and as a symbol of the National Socialist Party. For Hitler, it was an integral part of Germania, his new World Capital. It formed part of the Southern end of the North-South axis of Speer's urban plan. Tempelhof was also one of the few projects of Germania which was actually realised, and it gives a sense of the scale in which Germania was planned: covering some 200 000 square meters, the main airport building is still one of the world's largest buildings.

After the war, the airport ended up in the Western Zone, which eventually became West Berlin. The relationship between the Soviets and the West soon became frosty and paranoid. In an attempt to gain control over the isolated West Berlin, the Soviet Union closed all overland lines of supply to the city. All supplies had to be flown in to Tempelhof airport and for almost a year, during the Berlin Blockade, roughly 200 000 flights landed primarily in Tempelhof. Eventually, the Soviets reopened the overland supply corridors, but Tempelhof became a symbol of the connection to the free world and of a triumph over Soviet oppression.

After the Cold War, Tempelhof remained active as one of the city's three airports. West Berlin had developed the larger Tegel airport in the 1960's and East Berlin used the former military airport

Schönefeld. Both of these had longer runways and were located outside the major residential areas, and as a result, Tempelhof was only used for short-haul domestic flights. The only international flight was a weekly run to Brussels, used primarily by commuting Members of the European Parliament, lending Tempelhof the reputation of an airport for the rich. In a referendum in 2009, the vote to close the historic airport was approved by a small margin.

When Tempelhof shut down, there were still no plans as to what to do with the site. Under most circumstances, 200 hectares of prime real estate in the middle of a large European city usually means big money. Berlin, however, is different. Land is quite cheap as it is, and the city already has a surplus of land and housing. The historic nature of the airport, primarily focusing on its role during the Berlin Blockade, renders it a central historic relic that cannot be tampered with without massive protests. So far, at least two architectural competitions have been held, trying to find a feasible solution for the combination of a massive relic, profitable development and a park that will make everybody happy.

The most recent competition focused on the interesting task of merging Tempelhof with the city while conserving its historical aspects. It is most likely that the airport will gradually be absorbed by the urban fabric, but by preserving certain features, such as the taxi-ring and the two runways, the hope is that the relic will merge with the city in a way which will not only encourage the area's development, but also carry Tempelhof over in the future urban fibre as remaining readable traces. The same approach has been taken with the remains of the Berlin Wall, but with less successful results – although the rapid disappearance of traces of the Wall is admittedly almost certainly due to the fact that the structure is burdened with heavy negative associations.

The process of historical relics being absorbed and yet having their shape preserved is by no means unique to Berlin. This type of evolution and preservation of form is common to most old cities. Take for instance central London, a good example since London is a city with a long continuous history. Almost any straight road in London is Roman in origin, while most other roads demarcate the former borders between farmers' fields from the 8th Century.

Thus, you can read a 1300 year-old farm landscape in the pattern of today's urban fabric. Normally, the process is the result of an ad hoc development over centuries, where the replacement of components is gradual and organic. As a city without historical continuity, Berlin is currently using this process to artificially manufacture one. The plan is for Tempelhof to weave itself into the urban fabric, to seamlessly merge and make an imprint on the layout of the future Berlin. It is a kind of hyper-real image of Berlin's history. History in the former airfield will speed up, and the process of assimilation into the urban fabric that previously took centuries will now take years or decades at most. It is a case of selective history, a case of controlled decay; it is also uncomfortably close to Speer's theories on ruin value. Tempelhof as a structure has a diverse history. And that is perhaps what will allow it to become a neutral relic; in a way Tempelhof is a relic of the entire 20th century, good and bad.

Images
p. 42: Nature reclaiming the the concrete surfaces
p. 44-45: Along the runway

Berlin's bunkers

Berlin is full of bunkers. Some are more visible than others and some have even become topography rather than buildings. Obsolete bunkers are relics that tend to remain standing regardless of circumstance; being difficult to demolish is as much a part of their nature as their ability to be camouflaged is, which makes them a series of half-invisible and more or less eternal relics. As a building typology, they have always fascinated with their secret nature – the fact that they theoretically could extend in infinity, right underneath your street, much like the catacombs of Rome or Batman's cave. Bunkers are largely a product of the last century: advancements in theories of camouflage and technological progress made them possible, and the evolution of bomb planes made them essential.

World War II and the Cold War demanded an endless array of bunkers, air-raid shelters and other protective structures. The now peaceful Berlin is left to contend with all of those heaps of armed concrete. In by far the most cases, demolishing them would entail blowing up a couple of blocks in each direction.

Some underground bunkers have been filled over and forgotten. Hitler's *Führerbunker* belongs to this category. This was located underground close to the Speer-designed *Neue Reichskanzlei* (*The New Chancellery*) building, which was destroyed by the Red Army when they conquered Berlin. The Red Army attempted to blow up the *Führerbunker* as well, but it proved too strong to destroy.

In 1959, the East German government made a renewed attempt at demolishing it, but finally resorted to burying it after removing all visible signs of it. In the middle of the 1980's, parts of the bunker were uncovered during the construction of residential buildings in the area, but these were destroyed or buried again.

Right from the end of the war, there were fears that the site of the *Führerbunker* would become a Neo-Nazi shrine. There has been a continuous collective effort to forget its location and not only leave it unmarked, but also to keep its surroundings unspectacular and anonymous. In 2006, however, a plaque was set up at the site to dispel any legends revolving around the *Führerbunker*.

The conscious effort to understate and to forget the *Führerbunker* is an effort to speed up time, to artificially let the bunker and its site fall out of memory unmarked. Under normal circumstances, this a lengthy process, but here it has been accelerated with the assistance of bland architecture and anonymity. The surroundings are a conscious anti-monument dedicated to de-dramatising the historic site, and the plaque itself is an indication of the precariousness of ignoring something: it might be unremembered, but it might also evolve into a legend. Speeding up history is not without its risks.

There are many forgotten or sealed underground bunkers in and around Berlin. Another example is the *Bunker 17/5001* – the nuclear explosion-proof war headquarters of the East German administration, located in close vicinity to the village Prenden. Completed in 1983, the bunker could accommodate 400 people for up to 14 days. The bunker could more or less withstand a direct nuclear hit and was allegedly the most advanced bunker of the Eastern Bloc outside the Soviet Union.

After the fall of the Berlin Wall, the bunker became useless as a defence system, and the West German *Bundeswehr* sealed it in 1993 after removing and selling the diesel generators. *Bunker 17/5001* was repeatedly broken into and stripped of its copper wiring and other valuable scraps, and over time its location became a public secret. In 2008, the bunker was opened for visits for a short period of time. Through a temporary arrangement, visitors with hardhats could climb in through a ventilation tunnel and wander around with a guide. After this, the bunker was hermetically sealed.

Preserving the bunker was quite simply without economic feasibility. The refurbishment necessary to make it safe for tours and tourists would cost well above a million Euro. By sealing the bunker, it would remain intact for future generations to open up. The sealing here was a method of preservation, a time-capsule, intended to slow time down rather than speed it up. Almost every structure remaining from East German times in Berlin has met a similar fate. If there is any pattern, it is that relics are deemed too costly to preserve and the only alternatives available are destruction or burial.

Other bunkers were hidden in plain sight, camouflaged to resemble ordinary buildings. As these are often too solid to demolish, they are simply left in place, sometimes becoming part of the topography of Berlin. This is the case with the *Fichtebunker* in Kreuzberg. Originally a gasometer which supplied the streetlights of Berlin with gas from the late 19th Century, the *Fichtebunker* was converted to an air-raid shelter during World War II. The bunker was constructed to protect 6000 people, but as Berlin was gradually destroyed during air-raids, more and more citizens sought cover there. Towards the end of the war, the bunker sheltered up to 30 000 people during air-raids. After the war, the

bunker served first as a prison, then a hostel and finally a storage space for supplies till the end of the Cold War. The *Fichtebunker* was another structure too solid to be demolished and too expensive to be altered. In the end, it was sold to an investor who decided to treat the bunker as a topographic element, and simply constructed a little gated townhouse community on top of the bunker. The residents have access to the bunker below, which has become a cellar, or catacombs underneath their daily lives. This is a somewhat exaggerated example of how cities always have evolved, new constructed on top of the old – from essential defense structure to catacombs in just a few decades.

Another illustrative example of a bunker that became topography is the *Sportpalast-Bunker*, where a Modernist housing block that stretches towards the bunker simply straddles the construction as a bridge would a natural obstacle like a canyon or a stream. The two, the housing block and the bunker, make a very strange couple indeed.

The *Sportpalast-Bunker* has been refurbished as a memorial site and is now used by a nearby school for education on the history and atrocities of the National Socialist years as well as a venue for the school's art exhibitions.

Yet another example of adapting bunkers is the *Hochbunker* in Reinhardtstrasse. This was originally built to resemble a building from the air, and was recently converted by art collector Christian Boros to house an art collection, a vault of of sorts. The inside of the bunker was converted into a private art gallery and Boros built his own house on top of the disused bunker. The bunker here becomes the basement of the house, protecting the collection.

Bunkers' static nature contrasts with Berlin's otherwise dynamic history – hence, the discrepancy between a relic's life and the speed of history becomes more obvious in these rigid relics which cannot be destroyed or manipulated beyond their original intention. The bunkers' context is manipulated to either accelerate or decelerate time while the object remains fixed and intact. The city of Berlin bends around the bunkers as it attempts to (re)write its history.

In reality, the bunkers are some of the only fixed points in Berlin's architectural history. Based on these points and how the rest of the city (r)evolves around them, one could read a version of the city's history.

Images
p. 48: Honecker's work room in *Bunker 17/5001*, reconstruction
p. 50-51: The site of the *Führerbunker*
p. 54-55: *Sportpalast-Bunker*

The Topography of Terror

The *Topographie des Terrors* (*Topography of Terror*) is a curiously disturbing museum. The site of the museum and monument was formerly the location of the headquarters of both the military SS and the Gestapo during the National Socialist era. The block was razed to the ground towards the end of the war, with only the walls of the basement's prison and torture cells remaining as a reminder and relic from the past.

The razed site ended up on the border which divided East and West Berlin, and as a result, the Berlin Wall came to run through the site. The site's history was always well-known and an attraction for the curious right from the end of the war. Exhibitions of the site led to the discovery and excavation of the old prison cells. In the thawing political climate of the mid- to late eighties, a joint exhibition of the history of the site, including the cells, was held on both the West and East sides of the wall.

After the wall came down, plans for a more permanent exhibition prompted an architectural competition that was held in 1992 and won by Peter Zumthor, with an austere and sober piece of architecture. By the time the foundations had been laid, the Berlin construction bubble had popped. The project was considered too expensive and in 2004, the foundations were demolished. In 2006, another architectural competition was arranged. The architect Ursula Wilms of Heinle, Wischer und Partner won, and the completed museum opened in May 2010.

The permanent exhibition consists of two separate parts: the outdoors exhibition, consisting of the excavated cells, and the new museum building with an exhibition room and a library. The museum is a single-storey square with metal mesh in the façade which renders it opaque from the outside and transparent from the inside. The landscaping of the site is minimal, with coarse gravel covering most of the unused ground.

There are several unique aspects to this museum. The first is that it is the only museum dealing with the national socialist era on a historically authentic site –in other words it is "on location". All of the other museums and monuments dealing with the National Socialist atrocities are located on neutral ground, to the extent that such ground can be found in Berlin. In other words, it is a relic converted to a monument.

The architects describe their concept as a focus on the land: "the land is the first exhibit", while the building avoids attempting any interpretation of the site and its history, instead leaving this up to the exhibition and the remaining prison and torture cells from the basement. In that sense, it is a monument pretending to be a relic, borrowing authenticity from the historical site.

Another unique aspect of this museum is that it is the first museum dedicated to the criminals rather than the victims of the Nazi terror. Countless large and small monuments throughout the city of Berlin focus on the wars' victims; this is the only one that focuses on the Nazi war criminals and how the democratic and ambitious Weimar Republic could become one of the darkest regimes in human history in less than a decade.

Contemporary monuments dealing with the Nazi past are becoming ever more abstract, and the Topography of Terror is perhaps the most abstract to date. The building is not only devoid of symbols but of expression altogether; almost even of permanence. Strangely, the language of monuments attempting to address Germany's dark past appears to be evolving into a more and more abstract jargon over time.

How can the horrors of the 20th century be appropriately represented as monuments? Constructing monuments in contemporary Berlin is a complex balancing act. The primary fear is inadvertently building something that could potentially serve as a shrine for the neo-Nazi movement. This causes a strange tension between memorials and the eradication of relics.

In general, the policy has been to remove any relics of the National Socialist past which are loaded with symbolism. The demolition of the *Kriegsverbrechergefängnis Spandau* (*Spandau Prison*), which contained sentenced Nazi war criminals, is an example of this. In other instances, like the *Führerbunker*, the surroundings are kept anonymous and unromantic, marked only with a small plaque to ward off myths and legends from the site. It is a strange balance between remembering the past, keeping it alive, and distancing the present from the past through the destruction of physical remnants. In the case of the *Topography of Terror*, the result is a curiously cold and anonymous museum.

The other balancing act is between the need to build memorials and monuments to address the past and the fear of the city becoming a Nazi theme park for tourists. Often, tourists come to Berlin in search of the macabre Nazi past, with a complete lack of appropriate sensibility for the delicate situation in which today's

Germans find themselves. The tourist industry is currently the fastest growing industry in Berlin, but Berlin resists cashing in on this type of tourism and getting stuck in its own past.

This is the background to the site's ambivalently anonymous and almost ephemeral museum. A precautionary brief for the architectural competition called for a museum that was as neutral as possible, an anti-monumental building that would avoid becoming a symbol in itself. The monuments are intended to serve as an anonymous reminder, austere and simultaneously impermanent, abstract yet symbolic; such are the monuments of contemporary Berlin. Perhaps it is a necessity, but the question of the appropriateness of this strategy in a monument focusing on Nazi war criminals remains.

Images
p. 58: The empty atrium of the Topography of Terror Museum
p. 60-61: The site and the museum of the Topography of Terror

The Holocaust Memorial

The *Denkmal für die ermordeten Juden Europas* (*Memorial to the Murdered Jews of Europe*) or the *Holocaust-Mahnmal* (*Holocaust Memorial*) in central Berlin was designed by American architect Peter Eisenman and opened in 2005. Located on the former *"Death Strip"*, the monument spans almost two hectares and consists of a landscape of 2711 concrete plinths – the number of pages in the Talmud. The plinths are placed out on a regular grid and are all slightly inclined. Their heights vary from level with the ground to five metres, but the level of the Cartesian grid on the ground varies as well, producing a space in between them that physically evokes an array of feelings and impressions. The landscape is a very powerful memorial.

The memorial was first conceived of in the late 1980's. When the Berlin Wall came down, its construction quickly became a matter of national importance. The united Germany set up its capital in Berlin, the former capital of the Third Reich, and the reunited Berlin felt it needed to deal with its past in the form of a monument, one for each of the groups persecuted by the Nazis: Jews, homosexuals and the Roma and Sinti. The design competition held produced over five hundred proposals; from these, the jury selected thirteen. The majority were very harsh and literal reminders of the Holocaust, where names of extermination camps would be projected by the sunlight onto the visitors, or where the names of the victims would be inscribed in stone. In the end, Peter Eisenman's abstract proposal emerged as the winner.

The *Holocaust Memorial* is a spatial monument. According to Eisenman, the monument is meant to evoke the feeling of an ordered system that has lost touch with human reason. From the outside, the monument appears navigable and comprehensible, but once inside, its rolling landscape and imposing plinths become confusing and almost terrifying. The way the plinths divide the space, limiting your vision to four angles at any given moment, adds to the sense of dislocation, making it easy to feel threatened and disoriented inside.

Documentation states that the memorial has been deliberately left devoid of interpretation and is intended to be an abstraction, leaving the interpretation open to the visitor. Monuments, however, are never constructed without intentions, without purpose and without interpretations. Especially not this one.

On the one hand, the *Holocaust Memorial* is a *Mahnmal*, a warning reminder to future generations of past atrocities. However, monuments have wider functions. A monument takes things out of the present and places them firmly in the past, in the history books. A monument always creates a distance between the event to be remembered and the present, and thus, monuments can not only be created to remember, but also to forget. In a sense, erecting a monument is putting memory into stone: not only solidifying the memory, but also relieving the human mind. Guilt and anxiety are transferred into the stone so that the human mind can move on and leave the horrors behind. This is intrinsic to the concept of the *Mahnmal*. It is simultaneously a monument of remembrance and of forgetting. One guidebook to Berlin calls the *Holocaust Memorial* a graveyard, a final resting place for the confrontation with the Nazi past.

This is the unavoidable dual nature of the *Mahnmal*. The *Mahnmal* creates a point that says: this is history, let us always remember it and let us get on with our present and leave the past where it belongs – in the past.

The dual nature of the *Mahnmal* is in a sense assisted by the abstraction. The lack of symbols distances the monument further from the context, rendering it almost timeless. This timelessness through abstraction will on the other hand also keep it relevant and current. Symbols age differently, while the faceless *Holocaust Memorial* is strong enough to survive on its own, without symbols.

A debated aspect of the *Holocaust Memorial* is the singling out of Jewish people from among the many groups that were persecuted by the Nazis. According to some of the monument's critics, this creates a hierarchy of victims. These critics furthermore claim that the division into specific groups was a Nazi practice, where people were assigned value according to which group they belonged, and to continue this tradition is madness; all of the Holocaust's victims were human beings and that is the essence of what we can learn from history.

The plan has been to build a monument to each of the persecuted groups. A memorial to murdered homosexuals has recently been completed, and another for murdered Roma and Sinti is currently planned. *The Denkmal für die im Nationalsozialismus verfolgten Homosexuellen* (*Memorial to Homosexuals persecuted under Nazism*) consists of one gigantic plinth almost hidden away in the park Tiergarten, across the street from the *Holocaust Memorial*. The plinth is hollow, and inside a looped video shows two men engaged in a kiss.

Where the *Memorial to the Murdered Jews* is abstract and spatial, the *Memorial to Homosexuals persecuted under Nazism* is very concrete, connecting the past to the present, with a plaque describing contemporary persecution of homosexuals around the world.

Perhaps the most interesting monument is the one that has not yet been completed: the *Denkmal für die im Nationalsozialismus ermordeten Sinti und Roma* (*Memorial to the Murdered Sinti and Roma*). Construction of the monument, which is hidden deep in Tiergarten, was commenced in 2008, but has since almost been forgotten. In August 2010, it is still a construction site, which for all intents and purposes appears abandoned. The construction itself is in a tent. A sign, presumably announcing the planned monument to the outside, has been obstructed by a wall that hides the construction site from public view. This stalled construction is perhaps the most important monument of them all, the one which forces us to reflect on whether or not we have learnt anything from this horrible period in human history.

The crimes committed against the Jewish people are well acknowledged, and great sympathy has been extended over the last half century to Jewish people from across the world. The crimes against the Roma and Sinti often seem to be have been forgotten. Discrimination against the Roma and Sinti is still rampant across Europe, much as it was against Jews before the war. Europe is taking an ever harder stance against Roma and Sinti people and during the last decade, special legislation that is horrifyingly similar to that of the Nazi administration has been passed in several countries, Italy and Eastern Europe in particular.

The *Memorial to Homosexuals persecuted under Nazism* has a form reminiscent of the *Holocaust Memorial*, to demonstrate that it is part of the same event. However, if you read the three monuments together, the gigantic monument to Holocaust, the small, but finished monument to the murdered homosexuals, and the monument to the murdered Sinti and Roma people, hidden away half forgotten in a little-used section of the park, it is arguably an illustrative trinity.

Images
p. 66-67: The *Holocaust Mahnmal*
p. 70-71: *Memorial to Homosexuals persecuted under Nazism*
p. 72-73: *Memorial to the Murdered Sinti and Roma,* current status

Endnotes

Berlin in the process of writing its continuous history is a fascinating place. Time speeds up and slows down alternatingly in different locations across the city. In some places, like Hitler's *Führerbunker*, time is sped up; these places are destined for instant eradication, both as physical and historical locations. In the case of the *Stadtschloss*, time appears to move backwards, and at Tempelhof history is progressing centuries in decades. There is no overall plan or scheme behind this; it is merely a very pragmatic way of dealing with history. It is a way of coming to grips with the past, rewriting a version of it with which everyone can feel comfortable. At most, there is a subconscious will to rewrite the past, a will to leave most of the 20th century behind and to manufacture an artificial historical continuity. It is the hyper-real nostalgia for a past that never existed.

It is exhilarating to be here in Berlin during the process. At the moment, everything is in flux, especially history and time, creating a dynamic city changing its future through cosmetic alterations of its past. It should be interesting to see what comes out of the chronological chaos through which the city is passing, whether this attempt will be successful and if historical continuity can be written into the urban fabric retroactively. It is a fantastically fascinating and unique experience to wander around the city and feel time alternatingly speed up or slow down.

The main question is how the future will view this moment in time. How will history itself adapt to Berlin's artificial historical continuity? Taking the liberty to rewrite past relics and monuments is nothing new. Napoleon did it, plenty of the Popes of Rome did it, and so did Hitler. In a sense, however, it is a way of writing yourself at the end of history, a folly upon which future generations might frown. But all things considered, this is probably what has always been done and how history is continually shaped: for reasons of nostalgia, pride and identity. History, in Berlin more than many other places, is very, very subjective. The city of Berlin is realigning itself with its history, and at the same time realigning its history through the city.

Images
p. 76: The Holocaust Memorial
p. 78-79: Potemkin village near Leipziger Platz

Part II

The informal relics of Berlin

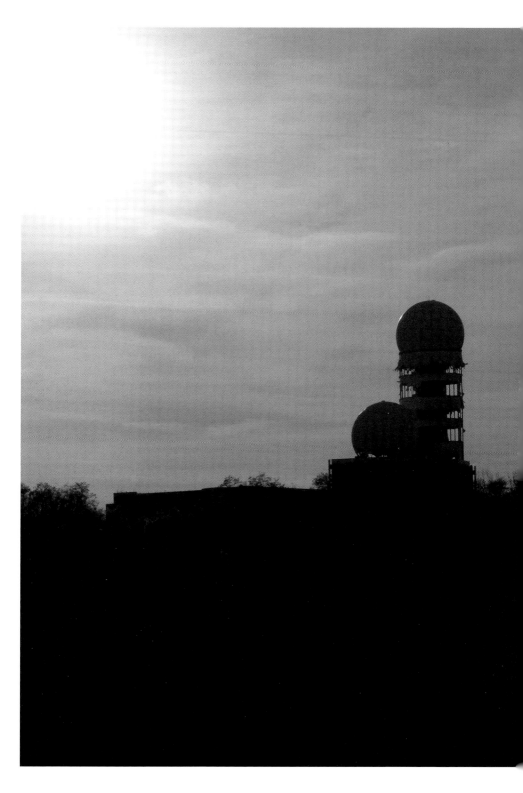

The history of Berlin is a history of conflicting systems attempting to realise their Utopian visions in an urban setting. The city has been a laboratory of built ideologies, each one treating their subject like a Tabula Rasa.

The conflicting systems have all left their imprint on Berlin, and while many have been forgotten, converted or destroyed, countless others remain today. Some are incorporated in the urban fabric, while others have become useless and obsolete.

Most of the relics here are from the turbulent 20th century, and primarily period remains from the National Socialist years and the Cold War era. The conscious relationship to relics of the NS period has understandably erased most of the remaining structures from these years. Some, like the North-South *S-Bahn Tunnel*, which was part of the plans for Germania, have simply been absorbed into the city's urban fabric. The Olympic Village is among the more interesting relics left from this era. It has been de-politicised through its focus on the sportsmen, in particular Jesse Owens.

Berlin's relationship to Cold War relics is much more complex. The primary relic from the Cold War was naturally the Berlin Wall, which continues to define Berlin to a great extent even in its absence. Berlin had an abundance of instant Cold War relics on both sides of the Wall, when it fell: instantly useless structures that were abandoned, modified, demolished or simply ignored.

Today, most of the more famous relics are gone or have been turned into monuments. The *Palast der Republik* (see Part I of this book) and most of the Berlin Wall have all but vanished. To a great extent, the defining structures of East Germany have disappeared. In West Berlin, it was not administration or government buildings that became obsolete, but primarily military structures, incredibly strategically important one day, well-nigh worthless the next.

While most of the famous structures of the Cold War have dematerialised, many remain, often hidden away. Some are public secrets and popular destinations for excursions and explorations, while others are consigned to oblivion. The informal relics all have captivating histories, and their existence is often a by-product of either the division or, almost as often, the reunification.

This section focuses on the informal relics of Berlin and how they came to be, their role in the contemporary city and what they have come to symbolise. These are but a few traces of the division, a few of the spaces that lost importance after the Wall came down. There are innumerable others, each with their own story.

Images
p. 82: The radar tower of the abandoned American Army base

The voids of the Berlin Wall

It is impossible to write about Berlin without including the former Berlin Wall. The Wall that separated the East from the West for twenty-eight years, from 1961-1989, officially ceased to exist over twenty years ago, but it still plays a central role in the city. When the Wall came down, the general opinion was that it should be excised from Berlin, from history and from the minds of the city's inhabitants. The question of preservation was secondary to the desire for reunification, and voices asking the city to preserve stretches were raised only very late in the euphoric beginning of the 1990's.

As it has turned out, the physical wall has become a ghost. A conscious policy to rebuild Berlin from Potsdamer Platz to Bernauer Strasse and the wish to conceal the city's unsightly scars have led to the removal most of the actual Wall. As the Wall was superimposed on an already existing city – which has since been reconstructed – it can be difficult to trace the Wall on a map today, while in the actual landscape, especially some distance away from the most central parts, many signs of the Iron Curtain's physical manifestation can still be seen.

Many have written about the Wall, what it meant to Berlin as a monument and what it has continued to symbolise for Berliners. One aspect of particular interest is the significance of the physical void left behind by the Berlin Wall.

The voids of the former "death strip" have done more for the integration of the reunited city than any of the grand projects such as Potsdamer Platz, Spreebogen or the like. Today, the voids are what characterise Berlin and constitute the one of the city's prime assets. One could even say that the voids define Berlin culturally. Architect Rem Koolhaas was fascinated by the voids when the Wall was still standing, and wrote the now-famous words 'where nothing exists, everything is possible'.

It has now been twenty years since the Berlin Wall fell, the Iron Curtain was lifted and Berlin became one city again. During the first few years after the Wall came down, investments were made in the reunited city on a scale that rarely has been rivalled in Europe. At some point however, Berlin ran out of money and the city has been struggling economically since. Construction has continued, albeit on a smaller scale. Many of the new projects are constructed on land where the Wall used to run.

To some, the void left after the Wall is a scar which can't be concealed rapidly enough; as long as the scar is visible, the division of Germany and the inequalities resulting from the unification remain contemporary. These memories can't be written into the history books as *past* until the void has been filled. As long as the wound is open, the past will continue to leak into the present.

Architect Daniel Libeskind saw the physical voids as akin to mental voids in the collective mind, the marks of a society broken and a representation of the relationship between Germany and its Jews that was destroyed in the Holocaust. He maintained that the psychological voids would remain even if the physical voids were filled with new buildings.

The Wall was the millstone around Berlin's neck, but through its demolition, this symbol of oppression became the stage for freedom. The cultural capital Berlin has evloved into since the end of the Cold War would be unthinkable without the voids; this is where nightclubs, art-installations, concerts and flea markets thrive(d) to make Berlin what it is today. These spaces can be used for anything or for nothing. Experimental culture can burgeon and evolve. For all intents and purposes, these 'unprogrammed' spaces are the cornerstones of cultural innovation in this city.

The voids give Berlin a distinctive spatial character and create unique opportunities in regard to public space. The voids are free spaces, to be used or inhabited in different ways as long as they are of a temporary nature. The voids are a by-product of the Wall, perhaps the only positive one. If we decide that the voids of Berlin are spatial relics, they are no longer functionless empty spaces. On the contrary: they become spaces worthy of preservation.

Another aspect of the Wall is the layer of activity and function it now creates on top of the reunited city. An almost invisible line crisscrossing through the city, the former path can be – and is – explored by tourists and Berliners alike, providing a view of the city from a new perspective. Travel along the Wall's former path is best undertaken by bicycle and entails moving in an atypical pattern through the city, passing through neighbourhoods which would otherwise remain unseen.

Is the Wall today an relic or a monument? The voids are definitely relics, while the preserved stretches are monuments; they are authored in the sense that they are interpreted rather than objective, telling a story rather than just left as they were.

The museums and preservation zones are monuments, encoded with messages and interpretations. There are three separate permanent Wall exhibitions filling different functions in the city to date.

The *"Gedenkstätte Berliner Mauer"* on Bernauer Strasse is concerned with the preservational aspect, meticulously tending a section of the Wall and the former death strip and remembering its victims.

Perhaps the most famous preservation zone is the *"East Side Gallery"*, a section of the Wall which was converted to a gallery shortly after the Fall. Artists were invited to decorate a length of Wall in East Berlin which had previously been free from graffiti. This section of Wall is more a gallery of street art than a memorial, and it tends to be the destination of choice for tourists, as the colourful murals correspond to their vision of how the remains ought to look.

The privately-run *Mauermuseum – Haus am Checkpoint Charlie* (*Checkpoint Charlie Museum*) focuses on spectacular escapes and escape attempts during the years of the Wall. It also offers an opportunity for visitors to be photographed with border guards and have their passports stamped.

The rest of the Wall is a relic, albeit one whose effects on the demographics and the social composition of different areas are much more in your face than the disappearing physical traces. The integration of the reunited city is slow, much slower than anybody expected, and even twenty years after the Fall, the demographic division remains.

Areas with high non-German populations are generally the areas that were just on the Western side of the Wall, dead ends during the divided years but today quite central areas – for example Wedding, Kreuzberg or Neukölln. Areas on the Eastern side are typically old and run-down, with a few exceptions. These areas were rapidly gentrified when the Wall fell and still host a large, floating, international population of artists, architects and creative migrants.

To preserve the void as a common territory and acknowledge the unique spatial conditions with which Berlin's turbulent history has provided the city would be a positive motion, creating opportunities which would eventually help Berlin out of its slump, or slumber. Berlin will never be as picturesque as other German cities, but it can offer a unique urban landscape of spatial opportunities unrivalled by any other European city.

Images
p. 86-87: Void next to the river Spree in Mitte
p. 90-91: Void near Alte Jakobstrasse
p. 94-95: Void near Bösebrücke, Bornholmer Strasse

A tale between two cities

In central Berlin, Kreuzberg, there is a small ramshackle building that looks like it might fall apart any day. This is the story of this building, a story about a gardener who in 1983 decided to turn a small 150 square metre wasteland next to the Berlin Wall into his private fruit-garden – and somehow managed to get away with it in one of the most militarised and fortified urban landscapes in the world under the direct glare of two superpowers.

In the early 1980's, the Berlin Wall still separated the East from the West. The most dramatic manifestation of the Iron Curtain was this 140 kilometre long wall, which effectively divided Berlin into two separate cities, which developed independently of each other for over twenty years. Based on zones established by the Allies at the end of the Second World War, the Wall ran through the city with absolutely no logical relation to the urban fabric and lives of the Berliners. With only the Berlin Wall separating two paranoid superpowers equipped with endless supplies of nuclear weapons, tensions along the wall were often high- a wrong move might trigger a Third World War.

Like many other districts of Berlin, the districts of Kreuzberg and Mitte were separated by the Wall, which ran straight through a residential neighbourhood along a curved tree-lined boulevard. The Wall ran alongside this curve, and halfway along was a plot of roughly 150 metres square that ended up outside the Wall. Even

though it belonged to East Berlin this triangle was left outside, presumably in order to create clear lines of sight for the guards patrolling it on the Eastern side. East Berlin couldn't use the plot since it was on the wrong side of the Wall, and West Berlin couldn't use it since it was technically part of East Berlin, and thus it was left to rot.

Until one day in 1983, when a retired local resident of Anatolian descent living across the street on the Western side saw how the place just accumulated waste, decided it would make a great fruit garden, and simply appropriated it. At first, he used it only as a garden, but he later constructed a small ramshackle house on the plot. There was basically nobody who could stop him; the East German authorities could not or would not risk creating further political tension by interfering – and besides, his little house was outside the Wall. The West German authorities had no jurisdiction there since the land was technically located in East Berlin. At one point, the East German military came through the Wall to talk to the gardener, ensuring that he posed little or no threat to the balance of terror, but no further action was taken.

Today, the Wall is long gone, and almost every trace of it carefully removed. The little ramshackle house however, remains, looking more out of place than ever. Over time it has become an informal tourist attraction and the gardener, by now quite old, will show visitors around and recount his story for a small fee. Every time I pass by, I notice more and more tourists around, taking pictures of the little shack in the middle of the tree-lined boulevard.

The first important question is: what is the significance of this squat for Berlin today? It is a celebration of human ingenuity and entrepreneurship. The little building has the same charm as a little stubborn tree clinging to the barren wall of a canyon, where nothing is supposed to grow. It shows that against all odds, nature, or humanity in this case, can triumph, even over superpowers. In a way, it is an informal monument of individualism, of the triumph of the underdog – and Berlin likes underdogs.

Most of the local residents are very much in support of the gardener and his building. Berlin is a city with a lot of variation in its built environment. It is by no means one of Europe's more beautiful cities, but can at best be described as a city with endless variation in its architectural heritage. For many years, the government has attempted to heal the scars left from the division and devastations of the 20th century. One by one, they are disappearing to form an image of another, a newer and friendlier Berlin.

This leads us to the next question: will this little garden be permitted to live on? By now, the story, or legend, of the little house is so much larger than the building itself, and this is why it manages to remain. Without the house's very special history, it would most likely have been bulldozed a long time ago. Tapping into the tourist market by offering tours and interviews is not only a source of revenue for its occupier, but also a survival strategy. The more often this slice of informal history is retold, the better the odds are that the building will remain; it is already living largely on its own legend. Whether or not this will be enough to save it from future redevelopments and privatisations of the area remains to be seen.

Images
p. 96: The *Geçekondu* (Turkish for squat) along Bethaniendamm
p. 98-99: Front of *Geçekondu*

The Olympic Village of 1936

The 1936 Olympic Games were held in Berlin. When Berlin was chosen as the host city, it was the capital of the young, democratic Weimar Republic. By the time they took place, however, Hitler had seized power and treated the games as a massive propaganda opportunity. The most memorable part of the 1936 Olympics was however not the Nazi spectacle, but the four Gold medals won by the African-American athlete Jesse Owens, thwarting Hitler's attempt to make the Olympics a showcase of German superiority.

The primary relic of the 1936 Olympics is the well-known *Olympiastadion* (*Olympic Stadium*) and the adjacent swimming facilities on the Western outskirts of Berlin. The gargantuan stadium is one of the few major Nazi structures that have survived until now. Despite its refurbishment for the 2006 World Cup in football, the stadium's sombre Nazi past is still very present.

Almost forgotten, however, is the 1936 *Olympiadorf* (*Olympic Village*), located in the tiny village of Elstal, half an hour west of Berlin by train. It is laid out like a military camp in the forest, complete with barracks and the villa of the 'Commandant'. However, it is not modelled on a Roman military camp but instead a fictional German past, the barracks are not in an orthogonal grid, but dispersed in the forest.

The majority of the buildings adhered to what would become the aesthetics associated with National Socialism: pitched roofs, repetitive facades and asceticism in details. Interestingly enough, some of the buildings are modern in their expression. One of the central structures, the *Speisehaus der Nationen* (*Dining Hall of the Nations*) is decidedly Modernist, demonstrating an architectural ambivalence even in the early National Socialist years.

As soon as the Olympics were over, the site became an infantry school for the *Wehrmacht*, the German army during the NS years, and remained so until the end of the war. At that point, the Soviet Army moved in, removed any National Socialist decoration, and continued to use the old Olympic Village as army barracks. Over time, they started demolishing and replacing the old barracks with their standard barrack typology: pre-fabricated four-storey concrete buildings constructed perpendicular to the old barracks, but still following the overall layout. The Soviets left the Olympic Village in 1992, and it has since remained deserted, save for plunderers. The empty houses are now mostly shells, the National Socialist barracks are boarded up, and the Soviet barracks have been stripped of everything but their concrete elements.

There are refurbishment efforts underway for the Olympic Village, but it is a slow process as funds are scarce. It is also a politically dubious project, considering the general policy of eradication of National Socialist relics to avoid the creation of Neo-Nazi shrines. Here, however, the conundrum has been solved by appointing Jesse Owens the patron saint of the refurbishments. By focusing on his role in the Olympics rather than the political circumstances, the potential ghosts of the past have been exorcised. So far, the barrack of Jesse Owens, parts of the *Dining Hall of the Nations* and one of the sports fields have been refurbished.

In a sense, this is an alteration, and the refurbished Olympic Village will undoubtedly be a monument, interpreted and symbolising something else. For the time being though, one can explore the rest of the crumbling Olympic Village, the parts beyond restoration efforts where the ruins of two ideologies on the same grid are forever locked in a downward spiral of decay in an empty forest.

Images

p. 102: Abandoned Soviet barracks in the Olympic Village

p. 104-105: *Dining Hall of the Nations*

p. 106-107: Soviet barracks inserted into the Olympic Village

p. 108-109: The original 1936 Olympic Village and Soviet barracks

Spreepark

Hidden deep in the wild and overgrown park landscape in the southern end of the gigantic Treptower Park, surrounded by fences and patrolled by guards with dogs, rest the remains of *Spreepark*, a GDR amusement park that froze in its tracks and never started up again.

Originally, the park opened its gates in 1969 under the name of *Kulturpark Plänterwald*, attracting over 1.5 million visitors annually as the only permanent amusement park in the GDR. When the Wall came down, the amusement park was sold along with many other enterprises owned by the GDR regime. In the euphoria and construction boom of the time, nobody took the time to run a proper credit control on the buyer, a certain Norbert Witte. Witte had previously owned an amusement park in Hamburg, but was forced to shut it down after an accident which killed seven people. Things began well. The Spreepark pulled in almost 1.5 million visitors per year, but Witte wanted to change the park's visitor fee system from a fixed "flat-rate" entrance fee to a more western European "pay-by-ride" system.

As a result, visitor numbers dwindled, and towards the end of the decade, Norbert Witte was stuck with debts in the region of € 11 000 000 and very few assets. Under the pretence of shipping six of the main attractions to Peru for repairs, Witte made a run for it, taking his family and closest co-workers with him. In Peru, he set up a new amusement park, *Luna Park*, with the six

attractions he had brought from Berlin. After a couple of years, this failed, and when Witte attempted to return to Germany in 2004, he was caught with 167 kg of cocaine hidden inside the mast of the "*Flying Carpet Ride*". Witte himself was sentenced to seven years in prison, and his son is serving a twenty-year sentence in Peru for his role in the smuggling operation.

Witte's life has been made into a film, "*Achterbahn*" ("*Rollercoaster*"), and a musical theatre piece. The old amusement park has been left to decay, with nature rapidly reclaiming the grounds. Over the years, a few potential buyers have expressed interest in restoring the amusement park, but eventually backed out for various reasons. In the meantime, the park has become an informal relic attracting quite a few people. Urban exploration groups and just plain curious people flock to the park, which cannot be visited legally.

The story of the park is also the often forgotten story of the reunification. To the outside world, the reunification was the end of a dark century for Germany. But it was also the beginning of a long and arduous reconciliation process. The park could not work in the context of the reunited city; it could not readily make the transition from socialism to capitalism. Relics like the *Spreepark* remind us that the process is far from complete. With time, the economic differences between East and West will disappear, but it will take longer than most are prepared to wait. The *Spreepark*, at once a real and surreal relic, is a reminder of those for whom reunification was a failure.

> *Images*
> p. 112: The main entrance to the *Spreepark*
> p. 114-115: The Ferris wheel, visible from much of Berlin
> p. 116-117: This mysterious object is allegedly a cinema

The Berg of Tempelhof

Once in a while, the vision for a structure becomes so engrained in the collective mind that its virtual existence can almost be mistaken for physical reality. This is the case of the Tempelhof Berg; the image has become a virtual relic, even available as postcards and prints.

During the still-ongoing debate on the future of Tempelhof, an illustration of Tempelhof transformed into a 1000 m tall mountain suddenly started appearing everywhere. The creation of architect Jakob Tigges, the mountain was entered into – and quickly eliminated from – an idea competition as a politically critical, tongue-in-cheek proposal. Nonetheless, the strong illustrations found their way into newspapers, into the minds of Berliners, and on to the postcards pictured below. It can be found in the strangest of places: I recently saw it hanging framed in a bar among photos of historic images of the city. The idea simply resonated very well with Berliners, and it was viewed by many as an ideal solution for the old and disused airport.

The only problem is its construction; the newspaper *Tagesspiegel* calculated that in order to construct the mountain, 47 000 trucks would need to deliver 20 tonnes of construction debris each on a daily basis for a period of over five years. And then there's the question of whether the notoriously unstable ground could accommodate such an enormous weight. Even so, the traffic of trucks would clog the Berlin traffic apparatus for years, release

Berlin

untold amounts of carbon dioxide emissions into the atmosphere and create endless problems for the city and the planet. Not to mention the costs for a city so famous for its empty coffers that for a long while the city slogan, coined by former mayor Klaus Wowereit was: "*arm aber sexy*", poor but sexy. The mountain is a pipe dream, and everybody is well aware of this.

Relics often have a place in the collective mind even if they no longer exist; *Crystal Palace* is one such relic. Planned, future relics can occupy a similar position in people's minds. The Tempelhof Mountain, however, is a strictly virtual relic with no relationship to physical reality. It is the virtual world blurring the borders with the physical world.

The virtual relic is a product of digital culture. Photomontages and other credible visual evidence can easily be manufactured. Computers and digital culture also make it possible to disseminate convincing illustrations into the collective mind. By presenting an illustration in various ways, it starts to inhabit the mind, much in the same way effective advertisement places products in our subconscious. The digital culture allows the collective mind to separate from the physical world and enter the virtual world. The virtual world of our collective mind then interlaces with the physical world, creating images in our minds of things that never were, producing entirely virtual relics.

The connection between the virtual and the collective mind allows the virtual to seep into reality in unexpected ways. It creates a situation where the virtual and the physical approach each other and merge. When the virtual leaks into the physical world, we are seeing something entirely new. In a way, it is as if the collective mind of Berlin created its avatar, the digital alter ego that is all

Berlin wishes it was, and that avatar then started showing up on postcards and walls. In a sense, the postcards are from a new Berlin, where physical reality and the virtual reality are interlaced. It is not only the physical reality that merges into the virtual reality, but also the virtual invading the physical space.

The collective mind has previously produced hyper-realities, which have then been physically realised. Hyper-reality is the authentic fake, as Umberto Eco put it – the collective image of times past, for instance. Often this image bears little resemblance to what lies beyond the surface.

The future of Tempelhof is still undefined, but it should be interesting to see for how long the virtual history will run parallel to the actual history, at which point these again will be detached from each other and the mountain reduced to the relics of the dream in forgotten images and dead pixels.

Images
p. 120: Two postcards of Berlin landmarks including the Berg

Teufelsberg

Barring the virtual Berg of Tempelhof, Berlin's highest point is the artificial mountain Teufelsberg. Originally an anti-monument, it was constructed in the late 1940's partly to bury a Speer-designed military school too solid to blow up without inflicting serious damage on the surrounding landscape and partly as a gigantic junkyard for all of the debris produced during the Second World War by Allied bombings and the Battle of Berlin.

The mountain ended up in the British sector of West Berlin following the division of the city. A joint US and UK military surveillance station was soon set up on top of the hill, listening to East German radio traffic and monitoring the air traffic of the Cold War until its end. When the US military left, they took all of their equipment, leaving only the buildings of the station standing. Now little more than an empty shell, it is still visible from most of the Western part of the city.

When the Berlin Wall came down, hundreds of previously invaluable military strategic sites scattered around Berlin became worthless overnight. Teufelsberg was one of them. The top of the hill is divided in two sections, one with the military base and the other a part of the recreational area of Grünewald. This half is a popular place for picnicking and kite-flying.

In 1996, the entire hill was sold off to private investors who planned to turn the hill into a luxury retreat. As a part of the scramble to

rebuild the reunited city, the hill was sold at far below market value. Construction was delayed and in 2004, the city rezoned the area as "forest".

The investors sold the mountain to film director David Lynch and a German guru called Emanuel Schiffgens, head of the *Maharishi Peace Foundation*. At a public meeting in Berlin in November 2007, the two officially announced their acquisition of Teufelsberg: David Lynch in a suit and Emanuel Schiffgens donning a white robe and a golden crown took the stage and declared their intention to construct a transcendental university on Teufelsberg with the goal of making Germany invincible. The meeting got out of hand, especially when Schiffgens was asked what he meant by an 'invincible Germany', and replied "An invincible Germany is a Germany that's invincible". Things took a turn for the worse when Schiffgens responded to the accusation that Hitler had had the same ambition with the words "Yes, but unfortunately he didn't succeed." The meeting ended quickly afterward.

The hill was built from the rubble that resulted from the last attempt to create an invincible Germany. The new zoning status of the hill as forest will prevent construction indefinitely as there was no planning permission for the 'invincible university', and the authorities have stated that they will never grant permits for this purpose. Technically, the hill is still owned by the *Maharishi Peace Foundation*. A symbolic first stone was allegedly laid for the university.

There is a group of US veterans campaigning to turn the hill into a monument, but they haven't been successful to date. Berlin's complex administration rules require a primary appeal to the local authorities of Charlottenburg-Wilmersdorf, who refuse to grant any planning permission for the site. The next level up is the City of Berlin, who does not prioritise the issue at this point in time, seeing as any change in the current status quo will result in massive political protests, especially when the *Maharishi Peace Foundation* is involved. Since Berlin is not only a city but also a state in the Federal Republic of Germany, it has a Senate that could technically influence the current situation by declaring the site a historical monument. At the moment, it appears that all of these instances consider the present situation unsatisfactory, but are disinclined to take any action.

Teufelsberg has become an informal tourist attraction and a popular destination for weekend outings. The empty shell of the former radar-base is surrounded by two separate barbed wire fences. Since the station is unmanned, countless urban explorers, party organisers and people of a curious nature have cut through the fences, leading to a fence that bears witness to the history of the struggle between civilians and authorities – today, the fence consists primarily of mended patches upon mended patches upon mended patches.

The radar station itself is appropriate to its current status: it is, after all, named *Devil's Mountain*, it was built on the bombed-out ruins of a city and a Nazi military school and is owned by David Lynch. The graffiti-covered shell of the buildings makes eerie noises in the wind, unexpected holes in the ground can present nasty surprises, and it's hard to help constantly looking over your shoulder when on the premises.

In some ways, Teufelsberg is a sad place, stuck in a stalemate and rotting away. But it is also a relic laden with history. It began as a way to destroy a Nazi military structure and became the final

resting place for many of Berlin's destroyed buildings. During the Cold War it served as a surveillance point and was then abandoned and de-militarised. It has been through several different turns in development plans, up to the *Maharishi Peace Foundations* ill-advised schemes and the public outcry they caused.

The public's reaction to the plans of the 'invincible university' is an indication of the fact that we have indeed learnt something from the horrors of the 20th century. The status quo seems to be a monument of recollection, a reminder to remember the errors and dangers inherent to fanaticism and blind faith. The history of the hill, its deadlocked status and the slow decay of the military structures provide a relic stranger than fiction and too strange for interpretation. Teufelsberg is a fantastic relic with a unique history. In its current state of decay it expresses more about Berlin than any monument or constructed narrative ever possibly could.

Images
p. 124-125: The radar tower of the abandoned US Army base
p. 128-129: Structures of the former US Army base

Endnotes

The monuments and relics of Berlin create two separate images of the city. The first image is that of artificial continuity. Through the creation of strategic monuments, coherence and homogeneity is slowly being constructed out of the urban mess that is Berlin, to a great extent omitting the 20th century, or at best distancing then from now. The (a)mending of history creates a city with a dynamic concept of time, alternatingly accelerating and decelerating and sometimes even shifting from linear to cyclical in an effort to rearrange the city's past. The subconscious longing for a mythical 'complete city' expresses itself in many ways, and the efforts to heal the scars continue. As of yet, it is unclear when – or if – time will return to its normal linear pace or whether the city will spiral deeper into chronological chaos.

Berlin as a city has never stopped moving. When the recession hit, the city went from producing space to producing history. Spatial development on a massive scale was turned into a selective development of history and the manufactured narrative of Berlin. Alas, compared to the richness of the city's relics and their stories, it is a rather unimaginative narrative.

This image of a manufactured history is mirrored by an image created by a number of relics from the 20th century; relics that continue to tell the history of Berlin as a discontinuous process, a history of opposing systems and revolution rather than evolution. The decaying relics of the 20th century form their own very linear

image of the city, its history and, most importantly, its people. While many monuments with focus on the grandeur of a fictional past and juxtaposed with the anxiety caused by the 20th century tell one history, the relics are telling many small histories – the combined narratives of the city.

The French philosopher Henri Lefebvre made a distinction between 'work' and 'product'. To him, the 'product' is the designed, the consciously created, while 'work' is built collectively and without a specific plan or design. In this case, the monuments would be 'products' while the relics would be 'work'. As the relics have evolved beyond the control of the authorities, or rather, as a result of the lack of control, they constitute 'works'. The relics present an image of Berlin as a city of people and their stories; they are the collective continuity of people in a disconnected, disjointed, chaotic city.

Combined, the two images provide us with a complex image of Berlin that is nonetheless far from complete. Berlin is a city of failed utopias, each piled on top of the last, with people living in between. The latest utopia of historical continuity is just one more Utopian project, and sooner or later it will join the others in the colourful urban fabric of Berlin. Berlin's history read through its relics and voids provides a more accurate history and image of contemporary Berlin than its monuments ever could.

Images
p. 132: Remains of the Berlin Wall, Friedrichshain
p. 134-135: Teufelsberg

Biography

Fredrik Torisson, Architect S.A.R./M.S.A. (b. 1976 in Lund, Sweden) has been practising architecture in Sweden, the UK and Germany since 2006.

He graduated from Lunds Tekniska Högskola (LTH) and is a member of the Swedish Association of Architects.

His first book, Embryos, was published in 2005 and is scheduled for re-release by Ratatosk in 2011.

He is currently living in Berlin.

Contact: info@torisson.com